CREATIVE DECISION MAKING

Using Positive Uncertainty

By H.B. Gelatt, Ed. D.

CRISP PUBLICATIONS, INC.
Los Altos, California

CREATIVE DECISION MAKING
Using Positive Uncertainty

H.B. Gelatt, Ed. D.

CREDITS
Editor: **Michael Crisp**
Layout and Composition: **Interface Studio**
Cover Design: **Carol Harris**
Artwork: **Ralph Mapson**

Copyright © 1991 by Crisp Publications, Inc.
Printed in the United States of America

English language Crisp books are distributed worldwide. Our major international distributors include:

CANADA: Reid Publishing Ltd., Box 69559—109 Thomas St., Oakville, Ontario Canada L6J 7R4. TEL: (416) 842-4428, FAX: (416) 842-9327

AUSTRALIA: Career Builders, P. O. Box 1051, Springwood, Brisbane, Queensland, Australia 4127. TEL: 841-1061, FAX: 841-1580

NEW ZEALAND: Career Builders, P. O. Box 571, Manurewa, Auckland, New Zealand. TEL: 266-5276, FAX: 266-4152

JAPAN: Phoenix Associates Co., Mizuho Bldg. 2-12-2, Kami Osaki, Shinagawa-Ku, Tokyo 141, Japan. TEL: 3-443-7231, FAX: 3-443-7640

Selected Crisp titles are also available in other languages. Contact International Rights Manager Tim Polk at (415) 949-4888 for more information.

Library of Congress Catalog Card Number 90-84927
Gelatt, H.B.
Creative Decision Making
ISBN 1-56052-098-1

PREFACE

The first thing you need to know about this book is that the author has changed his mind. It's embarrassing to admit because I'm considered an authority on decision making. Like other ''decision experts,'' I have developed rational models, invented logical formulas and prescribed scientific techniques for deciding. I have even written a ''how-to-do-it'' decision-making curriculum guide for teaching rational decision making. The ''right'' way to decide was the ''scientific way.'' It seemed only logical to be logical when making up one's mind.

However, I have changed my mind. What used to be the way to decide, now isn't. It isn't because things aren't the way they used to be. Even science isn't what it used to be. But this is not a book on intuitive decision making or deciding from the gut. The rational, logical, scientific methods are not suddenly obsolete, they are merely insufficient.

What is needed now is balance. Today everything is changing so fast that it isn't wise to rely only on old formulas, standard practices, and limited models for deciding what to do. A balance must be found between always deciding by strict adherence to a scientific formula and always deciding by instinct. It isn't an improvement to be totally ruled by intuition over being totally ruled by logic.

I want to assure you, before you read on, that I am aware that everyone didn't always decide by rational logic, even when I was preaching it and when it was considered the conventional wisdom. People don't always practice what is preached. Mark Twain once said, ''Have a place for everything and put the thing someplace else. That's not advice, it's merely custom.'' He was pointing out that conventional wisdom often differs from common practice. People don't always do what seems the logical thing to do.

That's why this book was written. We need some decision advice that is more closely related to what people do than to what experts say they should do. In this book I'm saying, ''Have a logical process for making decisions and use something else. That *is* advice, and it *is* custom.'' However, the something else I'm advocating is positive uncertainty. Positive uncertainty is a balanced, versatile, whole-brain decision strategy featuring the creative tools of flexibility, optimism, and imagination.

(Continued over)

PREFACE (Continued)

This book takes on the challenge of bringing together the rational decision doctrine of classical science and the intuitive insights of modern science and places it into a flexible and balanced process for making choices today about tomorrow. Positive uncertainty will paradoxically combine intellectual/objective techniques and imaginative/subjective techniques into an unconventional wisdom for future planning and creative decision making.

For those of you who are worried that I might change my mind again, let me assure you, I will. Fortunately, this is a trait whose time has come. Changing one's mind will be an essential decision-making skill in the future. Keeping the mind open will be another. Learning to be good at being uncertain is becoming a modern-day asset in decision-making. The hard part to learn is to be positive about the uncertainty.

The equivocal advice of positive uncertainty, from an author who admittedly changes his mind, should prepare you to deal with ambiguity, guide you to accept inconsistency and help you to embrace uncertainty. Does it seem paradoxical to be uncertain and positive, to learn how to make up your mind and change it, and to become both rational and intuitive? Yes, but have you noticed that the future is full of paradox? This book recommends a balanced, paradoxical approach to making decisions about the future when you don't know what it will be.

H. B. Gelatt

ABOUT THIS BOOK

Creative Decision Making Using Positive Uncertainty is unlike most books. It has a unique "self-paced" format that encourages a reader to become personally involved and try some new ideas immediately.

Trying new ideas, in fact, is the main theme of this book. The reader will be acquainted with some of the concepts presented and will be introduced to some that are fresh and unfamiliar. Putting the fresh and familiar together is what leads to creative decision making with positive uncertainty.

Creative Decision Making Using Positive Uncertainty (and the other books listed in the back of this book) can be used effectively in a number of ways. Here are some possibilities:

—**Individual study.** Because the book is self-instructional, all that is needed is a quiet place, some time and a pencil. Completing the activities and exercises will provide valuable feedback, as well as practical ideas you can use immediately.

—**Workshops and seminars.** The book is ideal for assigned reading prior to a workshop or seminar. With the basics in hand, the quality of participation will improve, and more time can be spent on concept extensions and applications during the program. The book also is effective when it is distributed at the beginning of a session, and participants "work through" the contents.

—**Remote location training.** Books can be sent to those not able to attend "home office" training sessions.

There are other possibilities that depend on the objectives, program or ideas of the user. For more information on these possibilities, workshops, seminars or keynote speeches, contact the author as indicated on the next page.

ABOUT THE AUTHOR

H. B. Gelatt, Ed.D. is a speaker, workshop presenter, author, and consultant. His specialties are decision making, career development, counseling, futures thinking, and educational renewal.

H. B. received his masters and doctoral degrees in counseling psychology from Stanford University. He is a licensed psychologist in the state of California.

Following a successful career in education, H. B. has devoted his time to consulting, speaking, training, and writing. His clients have included the American Institutes for Research, the College Board, the Kellogg Foundation, the McDaniel Foundation, the California State Department of Education, professional associations, various educational institutions as well as numerous public and private organizations.

For information on workshop or seminar presentations, speeches, or training activities write or call: Dr. H. B. Gelatt, 30 Farm Road, Los Altos, CA 94024, (415) 967-8345. Your comments or questions about positive uncertainty are also welcomed.

ACKNOWLEDGEMENTS

First recognition and appreciations must go to my wife, Carol, for her creative ideas, skillful editing, and constant encouragement. She kept me positive through some moments of uncertainty.

My gratitude and thanks also to Betsy Collard, Program Director at the Career Action Center in Palo Alto, for her introduction to Mike Crisp and her continued reading, reviewing, and revising of many versions of this book which always resulted in improvements.

And a special thanks to Don Hays, Dale Burklund, Margaret Burklund, Glen Toney, Dick Carey, Joan Stanley, and Ward Winslow for their review and feedback on the various stages of the manuscript.

CONTENTS

POSITIVE UNCERTAINTY IS A WHOLE BRAINED APPROACH TO PLANNING YOUR FUTURE

A personal plan for making decisions about the future when you don't know what it will be.

A flexible, ambidextrous approach to managing change using both your rational and intuitive mind.

INTRODUCTION

> *The trouble with the future is that it isn't what it used to be.*
> Paul Valery

Life is a river and we each make decisions every day about how to navigate it. The way the river flows is changing. The river of the past was generally calm, somewhat predictable, and moderately manageable. The river of the future is more turbulent, usually unpredictable, and much less manageable. Our river is changing and our navigation should be changing. Life on the new river means we must learn, not only how to expect change and respond to it, but also how to imagine change and create it.

This book presents a new process, called Positive Uncertainty, for making decisions in changing times. *Uncertainty* describes the condition of today's river of life. The successful decision maker navigating the river needs to be understanding, accepting, even *positive* about that uncertainty. Today's world, like today's river, is constantly changing. Today's decision maker should be as capable of change as the environment.

A smooth river flowing through a flat terrain in calm weather is a linear system. Our linear scientific methods make it possible to explain, predict, and control the smooth river. By contrast, a turbulent mountain stream, where water splashes over rocks and twists around eddies, is a nonlinear system. Because the linear scientific methods of the past cannot predict the turbulent stream's chaotic behavior, a new science is born. The old science is not obsolete, just insufficient.

Nonlinear science (quantum physics) was invented to find order in chaos. We know how to make rational, linear decisions on the predictable, calm river, but do we know how to manage the extraordinarily complex, random parts of the turbulent river? We need some nonrational, nonlinear decision strategies. We need decision tactics for both steadiness and randomness; we need decision skills and attitudes to manage both order and chaos, stability and inconsistency. We need flexibility and balance. We hope you will find it in this book.

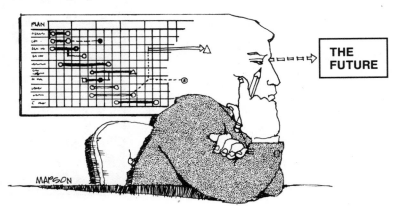

PLANNING THE FUTURE WITH UNCERTAINTY

It used to be that predicting the future was difficult; today even planning for it is hard. One reason that planning is so difficult today is that predication about the future has gone from being difficult to being impossible. In fact, almost 20 years ago, Donald Michael, in *On Learning To Plan and Planning To Learn*, concluded that social and organizational long-range planning was ''unfeasible'' because, among other reasons, the future is too unpredictable and people display limited rationality.

These two factors, the unpredictability of the future and the limited rationality of people, make organizational and personal planning unfeasible—*unless we change how we plan and make decisions*. First, we must accept, even embrace, two facts: the future cannot be predicted and people do not decide rationally. Then we need to change our approach from predicting the future to creating it, recognizing that the future is our present responsibility. Finally, we need to dislodge the superiority of rational over intuitive decision making because we need both strategies equally to make good decisions.

This book will tell why these changes are needed and show how they can be accomplished. The emphasis is on personal planning and decision making but many of the same principles apply to organizational planning and deciding. The main requirement for readers using this book successfully is at least a modest amount of uncertainty.

If you have ever thought, ''After I make up my mind I'm filled with indecision,'' this book is for you. Or if you have never felt uncertain about your choices, this book is for you. Uncertainty is an asset. It is a skill you can learn. The ''how'' part of this book features a modern, paradoxical philosophy of planning and deciding called positive uncertainty. The reader will learn to accept uncertainty as the condition of the past, present, and future and feel positive about this uncertainty.

MORE INFORMATION CAN EQUAL MORE UNCERTAINTY

Before radio, television, computers, and satellite dishes became common, life's decisions were often based on too little information. Today, technology has created an information glut. But the problem for decision makers is the same: uncertainty. To illustrate this paradox, let's look at your own decision making by answering the following questions:

1. Do you drink coffee?   ☐ yes   ☐ no

2. If yes, regular or decaf?   ☐ regular   ☐ decaf

      How often?   ☐ occasionally   ☐ often

3. List the reasons for your answers to the above questions.

_____

_____

_____

4. Is caffeine harmful to one's health?   ☐ yes   ☐ no   ☐ maybe

5. Is decaf less harmful?   ☐ yes   ☐ no   ☐ maybe

6. Will you drink coffee in the future?   ☐ yes   ☐ no   ☐ maybe

Many people make decisions about food consumption based on what they know about its affect on health. The reasons for their decisions come from what they read and other sources of information: advertising, research, or elsewhere.

The next page summarizes information from research studies on the effect of coffee on health. Read the summary and then answer questions 4, 5, and 6 again on the next page.

CHECK YOUR ANSWERS

INFORMATION FROM COFFEE RESEARCH

Is drinking coffee harmful to your health? The answer depends on how you make it or take it (the research, not the coffee) and on how much information you have and when you get it. For example:

- The *New York Times*, reporting several years ago, said that caffeine may both contribute to heart disease and help alleviate its symptoms.

- Later, a University of California (Berkeley) *Wellness Letter* said that caffeine raises, lowers, or does not alter heart rate, metabolic rate, glucose concentration, and cholesterol levels.

- Recently, a Stanford University study found that decaffeinated coffee caused a 7 percent increase in cholesterol.

- Another study by the Boston University School of Medicine suggests that five or more cups of coffee a day, regular or decaf, can cut your risk of colon cancer by 40 percent.

- In October 1990, a Harvard study of 45,589 men proved (sort of) that drinking coffee does not make people more likely to develop heart disease. Men who drank decaffeinated coffee, however, showed a slightly higher incidence of heart attacks and strokes.

- A spicy perk: the 1990 *Archives of Internal Medicine* reported that at least one cup of coffee a day keeps elderly persons sexually active.

Now questions 4, 5, 6 again.

4. Is caffeine harmful to one's health? ☐ yes ☐ no ☐ maybe

5. Is decaf less harmful? ☐ yes ☐ no ☐ maybe

6. Will you drink coffee in the future? ☐ yes ☐ no ☐ maybe

The research information on coffee drinking certainly provides grounds for uncertainty. Does it make you wonder if more information clarifies issues? Here is some other conflicting evidence from recent health research:

- The presence of asbestos, once said to be a dangerous threat to all of us, now isn't considered a threat to anyone except the workers hired to remove it.

- Fluoride was added to our water for health reasons years ago, but now we are told that it may be injurious.

- Today we learn that oat bran, the one-time breakfast table "miracle drug" against cholesterol, does nothing to reduce it in your blood stream.

The problem of deciding about coffee and hundreds of other daily choices is that you usually get incomplete, conflicting, irrelevant or even sometimes incorrect information. And once you've made up your mind, it's hard to change, even with new information. The new, ''healthy'' evidence about coffee will probably not reverse the downward coffee-drinking trend for two reasons: (1) the new evidence (caffeine is not harmful) can't overcome the old beliefs (caffeine is harmful), and (2) the power of marketing and advertising information is making cold cola the popular choice over hot coffee. Sometimes our minds change information when old knowledge blocks new knowing. And sometimes information makes up our minds for us unconsciously.

Research on health, of course, is not the only information you know and use in deciding about coffee drinking. The total sum of what you *know* is not the only basis for decisions. You also decide on the basis of what you *want* and what you *believe*. Now the plot thickens. And it thickens because of what we have learned about the powerful relationship between what we want, what we believe and what we know in making decisions. It is this powerful relationship that determines what we decide to *do*. It is partly what explains the unpredictability of the future and the limited rationality of people.

These factors are also why a totally rational, systematic, precise strategy is considered ''unfeasible'' for planning and deciding. Positive Uncertainty uses the four personal factors important in every decision—what we want, what we know, what we believe, and what we do—as a framework for its ''2 by 4 process'' of making decisions when the future isn't what it used to be and we don't know what it will be.

THE TWO BY FOUR PROCESS

Two Attitudes

1. Accept the past, present, and future as uncertain.
2. Be positive about the uncertainty.

Four Factors

1. What you want
2. What you know
3. What you believe
4. What you do

Positive Uncertainty uses these attitudes and factors to provide flexibility and balance. It does so by combining the traditional, linear, rational, left-brain approach with the creative, nonlinear, intuitive, right-brain approach and...? into an ambiguous, paradoxical set of principles for planning and deciding.

Traditional decision strategies say that when deciding, one should be:

- focused by setting clear goals
- aware by collecting relevant facts
- objective by predicting probable outcomes
- practical by choosing actions rationally

Positive Uncertainty suggests four creative, but paradoxical, variations on these traditional, rational procedures as modern, balanced principles:

- be focused and flexible
- be aware and wary
- be objective and optimistic
- be practical and magical

These variations are derived from the four factors and the two attitudes. They will become the four basic paradoxical principles of Positive Uncertainty. Following each principle is an example of a traditional decision maker who needs to become balanced in his or her decision-making approach. Do you identify with any of them?

FOUR PARADOXICAL PRINCIPLES

I. Be *focused* and *flexible* about what you *want*.

> Juanita was focused; she picked a target and concentrated it. The destination was the important part of life. "After all," she said, "if you don't care where you're going, it doesn't matter which way you go."
>
> She set her goals early in life. Juanita always wanted to be a CEO. Money and power were her objectives. She had the courage of her convictions. Changing goals and objectives was unthinkable.
>
> And then after years of climbing the corporate ladder of success, Juanita found out it was leaning against the wrong wall. By the time she got there it wasn't where she wanted to be. Juanita had money and power but found out she wanted entrepreneurship and a balanced lifestyle.
>
> Perhaps Juanita should learn to become flexible as well as focused.

Are you like Juanita? Where are you on this Positive Uncertainty continuum? Rate yourself by placing an X at the appropriate spot.

Very Focused　　　　　　　**Balanced**　　　　　　**Very Flexible**

1 ——————— 2 ——————— 3 ——————— 4 ——————— 5

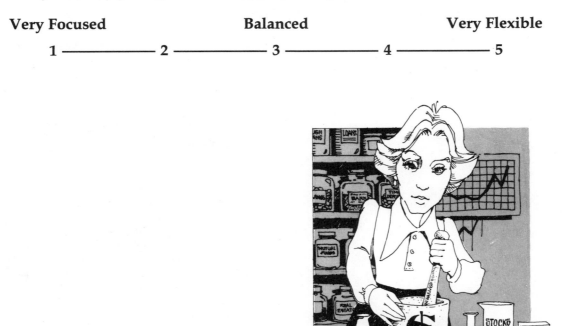

JUANITA: MONEY AND POWER

FOUR PARADOXICAL PRINCIPLES (Continued)

II. Be *aware* and *wary* about what you *know*.

Susan was smart; she knew what was going on. She believed that, ''What you know gets you to where you want to go.'' Getting information was important; in fact, she believed that having the facts was having knowledge. Susan did well in high school because she was good at getting facts. In choosing her college she used all the information sources: reading catalogs, visiting campuses, taking computerized college selection programs, and talking to alumni. When she made her decision she was aware of the facts.

After entering college Susan soon found out that information (having knowledge) before a decision was not the same as information after a decision. She found that information quickly becomes obsolete: the more you know, the more you realize you don't know, and there is no such thing as ''innocent information.''

Perhaps Susan should learn to become wary as well as aware.

Are you like Susan? Where are you on this Positive Uncertainty continuum? Rate yourself by placing an X at the appropriate spot.

Very Aware　　　　　　　　　　　**Balanced**　　　　　　　　　**Very Wary**

1 ———————— 2 ———————— 3 ———————— 4 ———————— 5

SUSAN GETS THE FACTS

III. Be *objective* and *optimistic* about what you *believe*.

Dave was objective; he was realistic about his future. He certainly wasn't going to be foolish about what he could accomplish and how much control he had over his future. His planning was always down to earth, with both feet on the ground.

Dave thought it was important to "see things as they are, not as I wish they were." When his wife's career promotion required a move to another part of the country, Dave knew it was good for her but bad news for him. He couldn't imagine being happy in the new environment. He probably couldn't find a job and he wouldn't be good at making friends. Dave wanted to succeed but he was also realistic.

But Dave didn't realize that, in many ways, life is a self-fulfilling prophecy. What he would accomplish would be determined largely by his view of himself and his future. And in turn, how much control he took over his future would also be determined by these same views.

Perhaps Dave should learn to become optimistic as well as objective.

Are you like Dave? Where are you on this Positive Uncertainty continuum? Rate yourself by placing an X at the appropriate spot.

Very Objective   **Balanced**   **Very Optimistic**

1 —————— 2 —————— 3 —————— 4 —————— 5

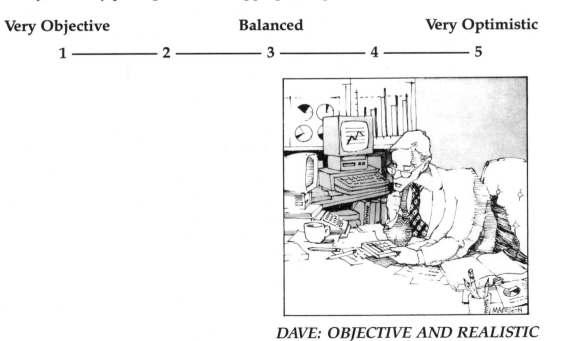

DAVE: OBJECTIVE AND REALISTIC

FOUR PARADOXICAL PRINCIPLES (Continued)

IV. Be *practical* and *magical* about what you *do*.

> Alan was practical; his plans and decisions were businesslike and methodical. He said, "I always make up my mind by using my head, not by the seat of my pants."
>
> When Alan made the important business and financial decisions in his life, he would rely on scientific logic, not on unreliable imagination. After all, he reasoned, the scientific method has been the accepted method for a long time. If it works, don't fix it.
>
> But Alan didn't realize that he didn't always use the scientific method, even in business and financial decisions, or that the scientific method was already being "fixed." A new science is now suggesting that intuition is not only magical but real. Two functional sides to every head (brain) are now recognized: a left side for rational thinking and a right side for intuitive thinking. Two heads are better than one.
>
> Perhaps Alan should learn to become magical as well as practical.

Are you like Alan? Where are you on this Positive Uncertainty continuum? Rate yourself with an X.

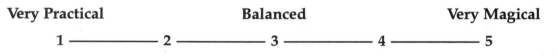

Very Practical   **Balanced**   **Very Magical**

1 ——————— 2 ——————— 3 ——————— 4 ——————— 5

Summary of the Four Case Studies

The four paradoxical principles balance the rational/logical with the intuitive/imaginative in human decision making, and they take into account what we have learned about how the brain works and how important attitude and beliefs are in determining what we do. *The minute you make up your mind that what you do makes a difference, it will make a difference in what you do.*

The new paradoxical principles also resemble more closely the way people actually decide. Although some people are better at left-brain thinking or right-brain thinking, most employ some of both sides when deciding. The needed skill in the future will be the ability to balance the two sides.

Next is a questionnaire to find out if your experience in making decisions matches what the principles are proposing. To find out, complete the questionnaire.

QUESTIONNAIRE: ARE YOU READY FOR THE PARADOXICAL PRINCIPLES?

Answer yes or no to the following questions.

___ 1. Have you ever wanted something, gotten it, and found out you wanted something else?

___ 2. Have you ever set a clear goal or a precise objective and discovered a better one along the way?

___ 3. Have you ever experienced serendipity?

___ 4. Do you sometimes engage in fuzzy thinking?

___ 5. Have you ever found it an advantage *not* to know something?

___ 6. Are you sometimes afraid to get a second opinion?

___ 7. Are you more familiar with the past than the future?

___ 8. Have you ever experienced misinformation?

___ 9. Have you ever distorted the truth?

___ 10. Do you sometimes feel unacquainted with reality?

___ 11. Have you ever found wishful-thinking to be an advantage?

___ 12. Have you ever experienced a "self-fulfilling prophecy?"

___ 13. Have you ever made an important decision in a way that wasn't totally rational?

___ 14. Have you ever decided not to decide?

___ 15. Do you find it is easier to be the result of the past than the cause of the future?

___ 16. Have you ever experienced clairvoyance?

TURN THE PAGE

RESPONSE TO: ARE YOUR READY?

If you answered yes to more than half of the questions on page 11, then your past experience says that a balanced approach to making decisions will be appropriate for you in the future. If you answered yes to all of the questions, you may already be there. If you didn't answer yes to any questions, please read on anyway.

The previous questions will all be discussed in the following section of the book which will elaborate on the four principles and provide ambiguous advice and a foolish formula for each one in order to help you learn to become creatively balanced in your future decision making.

Overview of Positive Uncertainty's Paradoxical Principles

#1 BE FOCUSED AND FLEXIBLE ABOUT WHAT YOU WANT.

- Know what you want but don't be sure
- Treat goals as hypotheses
- Balance achieving goals with discovering them

#2 BE AWARE AND WARY ABOUT WHAT YOU KNOW.

- Recognize that knowledge is power and ignorance is bliss
- Treat memory as an enemy
- Balance using information with imagination

#3 BE OBJECTIVE AND OPTIMISTIC ABOUT WHAT YOU BELIEVE.

- Notice that reality is in the eye and the I of the beholder
- Treat beliefs as prophecy
- Balance reality testing with wishful-thinking

#4 BE PRACTICAL AND MAGICAL ABOUT WHAT YOU DO.

- Learn to plan and plan to learn
- Treat intuition as real
- Balance responding to change with causing change

WHERE DOES POSITIVE UNCERTAINTY COME FROM?

Positive Uncertainty certainly is not the first or only recommendation for ambidextrous, balanced planning and decision making. The four paradoxical principles are based on the advice and views of other authors who have constructed such unconventional approaches as Fuzzy Thinking, Muddling Through, Mess Management, and the Technology of Foolishness.

Fuzzy thinking, a branch of mathematics, is defined as ''rational thought tempered by intuition.'' Wise fuzzy thinking is employed when precision isn't possible or desirous. Sometimes things can be clarified by making them fuzzy. Roger Golde wrote *Muddling Through*, the ''art of properly unbusinesslike management'' to bridge the gap between management theory and the realities of life in most business organizations. We need something to bridge the gap between today's decision theory and our realities of life.

Russell Ackoff, in *Redesigning The Future*, coined the term ''mess'' to describe the system of problems as understood by systems theory. Every problem is interrelated to and interacts with other problems (even a simple problem is a ''mini-mess'') but English doesn't have a suitable word for such a system of problems. Ackoff calls the management of these problems ''mess management.'' The four factors and four principles presented here should be thought of as an interconnected mess.

''The Technology of Foolishness'' is James March's answer to the overused technology of reason. Positive Uncertainty's paradoxical principles borrow from March's technology to offer a ''foolish formula'' for each principle and to present the idea of ''sensible foolishness to escape the logic of our reason.''

Bridging the gap between old theory and new reality may mean burning some old bridges and crossing some new ones. Which bridge to cross and which bridge to burn is a constant choice when planning your future.

PART I ▪ PARADOXICAL PRINCIPLE #1:

BE FOCUSED AND FLEXIBLE
About What You Want

> *Many men go fishing all their lives without knowing it is not the fish they are after.*
>
> Henry Thoreau

Remember the river of life? When you float on gentle waters you may be able to see your objective clearly and your choices may be well-defined. However, on chaotic rapids you might be forced to change objectives several times and be unable to consider all your options. To navigate both types of current skillfully, you need both focus and flexibility. Being focused and flexible is like being positive and uncertain. It is a paradox by definition: it seems contradictory yet might be true.

Check ☑ the following statements that you believe to be true.

Clear, precise goals can be an advantage because:
☐ They can focus your attention on your target.
☐ They can eliminate distractions.
☐ They can sharpen intuition.
☐ Other: _____

Clear, precise goals can be a disadvantage because:
☐ They can program your mind too narrowly.
☐ They can cause you to overlook unanticipated opportunities.
☐ They can blind your intuition.
☐ Other: _____

Is it wise to focus on clear, precise goals?   ☐ Yes   ☐ No   ☐ Maybe

Is it wise to be on the lookout for other goals?   ☐ Yes   ☐ No   ☐ Maybe

This ambiguous attitude about planning is explained in the word *serendipity* as described by Linda and Richard Eyre in their book called *Life Balance*. Serendipity allows you to discover something good while seeking something else. But this is not just a "happy accident." It requires that you seek something (be focused), and that you be receptive to something else (be flexible). Being focused and flexible may actually "cause" the serendipitous discovery.

GOALS ARE FOR GUIDANCE:

You want to be goal-guided, not goal-governed

Having a clear, precise objective and concentrating on it focuses you on the target. You don't easily get distracted or sidetracked. But concentrating on a clear, precise objective can be harmful because you may overlook other potentially useful options. The focused approach is best illustrated by David Campbell: "If you don't know where you're going, you'll probably end up somewhere else." But the following corollary illustrates the need for flexibility: "If you always know where you're going, you may never end up somewhere else." Somewhere else may be where you want to go but didn't know it. When events change rapidly, you can't be sure if where you're going or somewhere else is where you will want to be when you get there.

Rapid changes aren't the only reason for being goal-guided instead of goal-governed. People often don't know what they want until after they get it or don't get it. Many people strive to become what they become, only to discover that what they've become is not what they want to be.

Why don't people know what they want? What are some of the barriers to knowing? Check ☑ the ones you agree with and list others you can think of.

☐ Inadequate information   ☐ Pleasing others

☐ Lack of experience   ☐ Changing values/beliefs

☐ Unclear values   ☐ Changing information

☐ Changing conditions   ☐ Changing experience

☐ Other: _____

Knowing what you want has always been difficult. Not knowing what you want isn't a serious handicap; but if you think it is, it may cause you to pretend you do know, which *is* a serious handicap. To be balanced in setting goals means to be flexible about your focus. In other words, you can plan, but you should stay open to changing your plans.

GOAL SETTING EXERCISE

Let's look at a universal goal-setting question. What do you want to be when you grow up? The answer to that question is the basic career decision for every little boy and girl. The river of life is presenting some interesting new decision problems. Maybe we need a new basic question. What did you want to be when you were a child? Write down one thing you can remember:

_____

Are you that now? _____   Were you ever? _____   Will you be? _____

Has what you wanted to be changed? _____   Have you changed? _____

Many people are not what they wanted to be when they were young. This applies to career choice and other aspects of life. Things change and people change. And people change their minds.

Many people today are working in jobs that didn't even exist when they were growing up. List three jobs that didn't exist when you were deciding what to be.

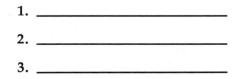

1. _____

2. _____

3. _____

People will change jobs 5–10 times in their lifetime. List the jobs you have already had in your lifetime.

1. _____   6. _____

2. _____   7. _____

3. _____   8. _____

4. _____   9. _____

5. _____   10. _____

When do you stop asking, "What do I want to be when I grow up?"

Are you grown up yet?   ☐ Yes   ☐ No   ☐ Don't know

Are you what you want to be yet?   ☐ Yes   ☐ No   ☐ Don't know

GOAL SETTING (Continued)

Of course, some people do become what they wanted to be when they were young. In fact, some successful, famous people knew what they wanted as children. It's not wrong to know what you want, but it's helpful to be able to change your mind. If you start out in calm water and later find yourself in the rapids, it's useful to be able to make changes. Sometimes when you find yourself in calm water for a long time you make your own waves to cause changes, to make life more interesting. Maybe the new basic career question should be, ''What do I want to be while growing?''

But how *do* you know what you want to be? How do you decide on goals? Making career and other decisions in life without clear goals seems foolish. But that's only because of past decision doctrine. Deciding on good goals should be compatible with the process of making good decisions. If wise decision making requires you to know what you want before you decide, how can you wisely decide what you want? *Wise decision making should be as much a process for discovering goals as for achieving them.*

In this way, decision making is seen as the cause of new experiences, new knowledge, new beliefs, and new wants. You make choices and you learn from the consequences. If you see decision making only as a means to *achieve* wants, not to *discover* them, you make decisions only after you know what consequences you want. Therefore, your wants are seen as the causes of your decisions, not the consequences. Shouldn't we be using a system that allows us to learn new wants as well as attain old wants?

Ambiguous Advice: **Know what you want but don't be sure.**

One way to know if what you want is what you want is to be unsure. If you remain unsure of your goals, you will be more likely to re-evaluate them frequently. The decision dogma, ''know what you want first,'' often causes people to pretend that they do.

PARADIGM SHIFTS

Another way to examine what you want is to look at the barriers to knowing. Remember the list from page 16. Too much or too little information can be confusing. Changing ideas and values can also be confusing. Many things are changing. For example, our image of the earth has changed, our image of the moon has changed, and our concepts of many of the laws of science have changed. Why then shouldn't our ideas of what we want also change? A good way to check if what you want has changed is to look at other changes. These barriers to knowing what you want are also the forces that change what you want.

For example, ''paradigm shifts'' represent changes in the way we see things. Maybe you are changing the way you see things. Your new perspective may in turn change what you want. The following exercise on paradigm shifts may help you re-evaluate your goals by looking at shifts in how you see things.

A Fuzzy Rating Scale

Since it is very difficult to be precise about such imprecise and ambiguous concepts as ''the way I see things,'' we'll use a ''fuzzy rating scale.'' Think of your wants, values, or way of seeing things, and try to indicate on the fuzzy rating scale of some general paradigm shifts where your are now.

Following are two sample ratings of the same paradigm shift using the Fuzrate technique.* After reviewing these two examples, inserts your fuzrates on the rest. Put an arrow at your preferred position on the scale. Then, indicate with a line how far left or right you are prepared to extend your rating.

EXAMPLE 1

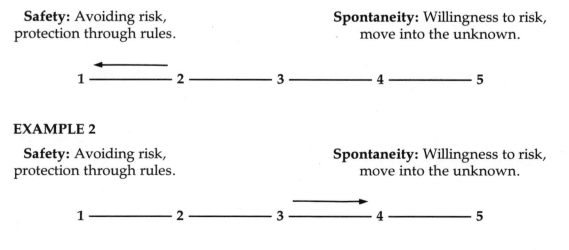

Safety: Avoiding risk, protection through rules.   **Spontaneity:** Willingness to risk, move into the unknown.

1 ——————— 2 ——————— 3 ——————— 4 ——————— 5

EXAMPLE 2

Safety: Avoiding risk, protection through rules.   **Spontaneity:** Willingness to risk, move into the unknown.

1 ——————— 2 ——————— 3 ——————— 4 ——————— 5

---

*from Pryor, Hesketh, and Gleitzman

RATE YOURSELF

Rating Paradigm Shifts*

Safety:

1 ——— 2 ——— 3 ——— 4 ——— 5

Avoiding risk, protection
through rules.

Spontaneity:

Willingness to risk, move into
the unknown.

Comfort:

1 ——— 2 ——— 3 ——— 4 ——— 5

Avoiding pain and threats to
belief system.

Meaning:

Willing to confront life as
contradiction and paradox.

Value information:

1 ——— 2 ——— 3 ——— 4 ——— 5

Getting facts, having answers,
being sure.

Valuing Insight:

Asking questions, accepting
uncertainty, eager to learn.

Permanence:

1 ——— 2 ——— 3 ——— 4 ——— 5

Honoring tradition, commitments,
memorialize the past.

Potential:

Change represents possibility.
Surprise is not feared.

*Adapted from Marilyn Ferguson

PERSONAL PARADIGM SHIFTS

You may find it useful to look at the personal changes around you in order to find possible paradigm shifts in the way you see things. Fill in the blanks, using your own sense of important changes. The first is an example or list below may give you some ideas but try to use your own impressions. Calculate your place on the continuum with the fuzrate technique.

Personal Paradigm Shifts

A.   **Dependent**   **Independent**

1 ——————— 2 ——————— 3 ——————— 4 ——————— 5

Compliant, subservient   Autonomous, self-reliant

B. _____   _____

1 ——————— 2 ——————— 3 ——————— 4 ——————— 5

C. _____   _____

1 ——————— 2 ——————— 3 ——————— 4 ——————— 5

Topics for possible changes in values, wants, ways of thinking.

Family	Quality of work	Power
Women's role	Self-help health	Economics
Independence	Profit motive	Evolution
Variety	Religion	Lifestyle
Education	Responsibility	Networks
Environment	Wealth	Politics
Relationships	Honesty	Leadership
Creativity	Prestige	Nationalism
Aesthetics	Altruism	

GOAL SETTING (Continued)

Foolish Formula: **Treat goals as hypotheses.**

Remember the guideline to be goal-guided not goal-governed. And the advice to know what you want but don't be sure. The old decision dogma allowed us to have doubts about almost everything except the thing about which we have the greatest doubts—our goals. So Positive Uncertainty recommends an experimental approach to goals.

One way to treat a goal as a hypothesis is to imagine achieving it. When you decide on a goal, the hypothesis is that when you achieve it, you will be pleased. The outcome will make you happy. You don't know for sure until it happens but you can experiment by imagining it happening or not happening or something else happening. You can even imagine not having a goal and finding out how that feels. In Positive Uncertainty, imaging is an important skill. If you are already good at imagery, try the next exercise: it will be easy. If you are not good at imagery, try the next exercise anyway: it won't be too difficult, and you will learn.

Imagining Outcomes Exercise

Imagine achieving some goal, wish, or fantasy. Imagine something that is real for you: a special vacation, a new home, job, promotion, house, car, microwave; or move to a different city, state, or country; lose 10 pounds; stop smoking; etc. If you can't think of a special goal, imagine you are spending a week in Hawaii: imagine all the details of every day, what you do, with whom, when, the weather, your feelings, other people, clothes, skills used, thoughts, fears, joys, frustrations, successes, failures, etc.

How did it feel in your imagination to reach the goal? Was the feeling what you thought it would be? Was it different? Can you imagine it being different? Was what you became what you wanted to become?

The mind doesn't seem to know the difference between what you experience and what you imagine experiencing. Therefore, if you have a good imagination, you can learn from a lot of imagined experience. Experiencing imaginary outcomes of proposed decisions is partial insurance against getting what you want and finding out it isn't. This means being unsure of your goals.

To treat goals as hypotheses does not mean to give up being focused. It means to be balanced. It's like having both a zoom lens and a wide angle lens. You need a target and you need to zoom in on it. However, if you don't also use your wide angle lens, you won't see the big picture, you won't see what else is going on. If you only use one lens you will only see the trees or the forests. A wise, creative, successful decision maker will need to behold both the forest and the trees.

The Case of Juanita

Remember Juanita who wanted to be a CEO. She was goal-governed, not goal-guided. She didn't treat her desire to be a CEO as a hypothesis. She was focused but she wasn't flexible. To Juanita, all of her career decisions were a means to achieve her goal. She didn't see them as a possible means to discover new goals.

While Juanita was climbing the career ladder of success, many changes were going on. The women's liberation movement, the entrepreneurial movement, and the technology explosion were causing some paradigm shifts in society's values and in Juanita's way of seeing things. Juanita fell in love, had children, developed an extended family, and moved to a new part of the country.

During all of these changes, Juanita was being successful in her career plans, and she stayed zeroed in on her target. Her clear goal and precise objectives programmed her mind so narrowly that she had a hard time changing it, even though she was changing. Juanita became someone who knew what she wanted but found out it wasn't.

In what ways are you like Juanita? What are your attitudes and skills in the what you want factor of decision making? Check ☑ the following answers that apply to you.

Personal Review

1. Do you think it is possible to be both focused and flexible?
   - ☐ yes
   - ☐ no
   - ☐ maybe

2. Do you think it is desirable?
   - ☐ yes
   - ☐ no
   - ☐ maybe

3. Are you best at:
   - ☐ knowing what you want
   - ☐ not being sure
   - ☐ being balanced

4. Are you best at:
   - ☐ treating goals as fixed
   - ☐ treating goals as hypotheses
   - ☐ being balanced

5. Are you best at:
   - ☐ achieving goals
   - ☐ discovering goals
   - ☐ being balanced

6. How would you rate your skill of assessing your goals by experiencing imaginary outcomes?
   - ☐ outstanding
   - ☐ adequate
   - ☐ needs to improve

Summary

Creative decision making using Positive Uncertainty recommends:

- Being focused and flexible about what you want

- Knowing what you want but don't be sure

- Treating goals as hypotheses

- Balancing achieving goals and discovering them

The what you want principle of Positive Uncertainty is paradoxical and ambidextrous. It is still advisable, even useful, to know what you want when looking for a job, buying a new refrigerator, or deciding what you want to be when you grow up. Setting goals and objectives is proper. Purpose before action, looking before leaping is still intelligent, even logical, behavior.

But, in a more turbulent society, this focused, reasonable practice needs to be supplemented with flexible, even foolish behavior so that individuals and organizations can act in the absence of a clear goal or change their goal in mid-stream. Not always. Not even usually. But sometimes. Sometimes you need to be able to do things for which you have no good reason. Or for the purpose of finding a good reason.

And sometimes you need to be able to change your reasons, to change focus. The best way to prepare for change is to be flexible. Does it seem paradoxical to be both focused and flexible? Yes, and that's what is needed.

> *"Not in his goals but in his transitions man is great."*
> R.W. Emerson

PART II · PARADOXICAL PRINCIPLE #2:

BE AWARE AND WARY
About What You Know

> *A man with one watch knows what time it is. A man with two watches is never sure.*
>
> from Murphy's Laws

"Be aware and wary" is advice both for what you know and what you don't know. Mark Twain could have been speaking about Positive Uncertainty when he said: "It ain't what you don't know that gets you in trouble. It's what you know for sure that ain't so."

In an information-rich society, what you know for sure today may not be true tomorrow. It is important to be aware of what you know and don't know. Information sustains our lives and work. The feeling is you can't be too rich or too well-informed. However, being well-informed may not be all it is cracked up to be.

Check ☑ the following statements you believe to be true:

☐ 1. Collecting all the information may paralyze you.

☐ 2. Information can cloud meaning as well as clarify it.

☐ 3. Information is in the eye of the beholder.

☐ 4. Information becomes obsolete rapidly.

☐ 5. Information is not always informative.

☐ 6. There is no such thing as "innocent" information.

☐ 7. There is more information available than one can process.

☐ 8. A little information is a dangerous thing.

☐ 9. Too much information can be a handicap.

☐ 10. You often get biased information from reliable sources.

BE AWARE AND WARY (Continued)

Information may be the sustenance of our lives but the 10 statements on page 25 suggest that what you know or need to know requires more than just having information. This is because information today is not always "user friendly." It is often misinformation: incomplete, biased, unreliable, irrelevant, subjective, and never independent of values, yours or someone else's. Every day you receive information that you didn't ask for, didn't want, isn't in your best interest, and is presented in such a psychologically persuasive manner that it is frequently used in your decisions without your knowing it.

How do you process all this information to make a decision? Positive Uncertainty defines decision making to focus on information processing: *Decision making is the process of arranging and rearranging information into a choice of action.*

This new definition has three parts: information, arranging and rearranging, and choice. What you do to make a choice is arrange and rearrange the information you get with the other information you already have and what you want and believe. Remember that information changes the mind and the mind changes information. In your mind you select, deny, filter, distort, exaggerate, project, rationalize, and repress information. Your mind scans, screens, and selects. It censors information from your perceptions of the moment and from distant memories. In this way you "use" information to get what you want.

Consider information and your decision about cholesterol. Mark in the space: True (T), False (F), or Not Sure (NS).

____ **1.** It is wise to control my cholesterol level.

____ **2.** Decaffeinated coffee increases cholesterol.

____ **3.** Oat bran reduces cholesterol.

What other information do you have about cholesterol? Write down some of it.

_____

_____

_____

Now try to think about what you don't know about cholesterol.

1. _____

2. _____

3. _____

It is hard to be aware of what you are not aware of, maybe impossible. But you can be wary. Your wants, desires, values, and beliefs about weight, diet, health, scientific data, and cholesterol all enter into the arranging and rearranging process in your mind. Sometimes this process is compared to how a computer works, but that is a false analogy.

The mind is not linear. It is not "garbage-in, garbage-out." Sometimes the mind changes the information. The mind can treat facts with imagination, the computer can't. The nonlinear mind is a remarkable instrument for processing. And it will not likely be replaced by computer robots because, as NASA points out, "Humans are the lowest cost, lightweight, nonlinear, all-purpose computer system that can be mass-produced by unskilled labor." However, humans need to be aware of how their minds work and be wary of how information is stored.

It all takes place right behind your eyes. You won't see it unless you tell yourself to look. Think about how you make your decisions about cholesterol.

Mark in the space: Yes, No, or Not sure (NS).

____ Do you have all the facts?

____ Do you have a clear objective?

____ Do you have some misinformation?

____ Do you know what you don't know?

____ Do you decide rationally?

These questions should make you think about how your mind uses information, not harass you about your cholesterol decisions. However, because our world is inundated with information and because we think we should be able to decide rationally, we often get anxious about collecting information and using it. But getting information and using information are two different things. In *Information Anxiety*, Richard Wurman tells us that a weekday edition of the *New York Times* contains more information than the average person was likely to come across in a lifetime in seventeenth-century England. This information glut creates an ever-widening gap between what we understand and what we think we should understand. It produces what Wurman calls information anxiety. Information anxiety is as likely to result from too much as too little information.

Ignorance is the best personal antidote to this anxiety, Wurman says. Being able to admit that you don't know is liberating. This leads to positive uncertainty's ambiguous advice.

BE AWARE AND WARY (Continued)

Ambiguous Advice: **Knowledge is power and ignorance is bliss.**

Having a mind full of knowledge is obviously a powerful advantage. But where knowledge doubles steadily and becomes obsolete rapidly, having an open mind is also obviously an advantage. An open mind is receptive. An unreceptive mind, even if it is full, is closed. This is the key to positive uncertainty. Ignorance is bliss because it is an ideal state from which to learn. If you can admit that you don't know, you are more likely to ask the questions that will enable you to learn.

Decision making can be divided into three parts:

1. The *actions* you could take: alternatives, options, choices

2. The *outcomes* of the actions you take: results, consequences, desirability

3. The *uncertainty* between actions and outcomes

This is what you want to know before deciding. This is what you don't know.

The ''What Else'' Questions

The decision maker has some information about options, consequences, and probability. However, if the decision maker were ignorant about these three parts, he or she could ask some useful questions. An open (persuadable) mind leads to open (suggestible) questions: ''What else could I do?'' (What other actions could I consider?) ''What else could happen?'' (What other outcomes might occur?) Think of this as personal brainstorming, where you set aside judgment and reality. Forget your previous knowledge; act ignorant. Try this series of practice exercises about actions, options, alternatives presented on the following pages.

Ponder Your Resignation Exercise

Imagine that you don't like your job and are deciding whether to quit. Resigning, of course, is one action you could take. Do you know all the other possible actions you could take? Assume you are your own decision consultant. Ask yourself the first "what else" question.

What else could you do? Think of every other alternative: rational, irrational, intuitive, mystical, moral, immoral, conservative, risky, practical, foolish, etc.

_____   _____

_____   _____

_____   _____

One of the most common pitfalls in good decision making is the failure to consider possible alternatives. Sometimes it's because you don't know they exist, sometimes it's because you know but "forget." Sometimes it's because they need to be created. Sometimes not knowing other options is OK; sometimes it's disastrous. As your own consultant, ask yourself, "I wonder what else I could do?" Be creative. You're looking for new territory; you want to increase your freedom of choice.

Many techniques help creativity. One such technique is Edward de Bono's six thinking hats in which each color represents a different kind of thinking. Try the above brainstorming exercise again six times, using a different colored imaginary thinking hat each time.

White—Objective	Yellow—Positive
Red—Emotional	Green—Creative
Black—Negative	Blue—Controlling

Perhaps you've seen that what you know is usually less than what you don't know. Being aware and wary keeps you positive and uncertain. This helps you be on the lookout for other actions you could take before you decide which actions to take.

Present Your Resignation Exercise

Now imagine you have picked the option, quit my job. What could happen? Think of possible outcomes and write them down.

_____   _____

_____   _____

_____   _____

BE AWARE AND WARY (Continued)

The Outcomes Window

What Else Could Happen?

The following technique, the outcomes window, helps the decision maker ask what else could happen and avoid the common decision mistake of overlooking some possible outcomes. It's a right-brained way to ask, ''What else could happen?'' It's a way to avoid surprises after selecting a certain course of action.

Every decision has four kinds of outcomes:

1. Positive consequences (gains) for you (''Get a better job'')
2. Negative consequences (losses) for you (''Feel like a failure'')
3. Positive consequences (gains) for others (''Wife sees me more'')
4. Negative consequences (losses) for others (''Less income for kids'')

Remember that outcomes include both events (getting another job) and feelings (happy, sad, guilty). The window method makes sure you think of all four kinds of possible outcomes. Fill in all four sections of the outcomes window for the possible outcomes of quitting your job.

THE OUTCOMES WINDOW

	POSITIVE	NEGATIVE
S E L F		
O T H E R S		

Review your completed window. Remember you're looking for insight.

1. Notice if some parts of the outcomes window are less full than others. If so, why? They could all be full if you worked on it more.

2. Was it easier to think of positive or negative outcomes? Why?

3. Who were considered others?

4. Which is more important, outcomes to you or to others?

5. Try to rate the positives and negatives in terms of desirability.

6. Try to rate the positives and negatives in terms of probability.

7. You can play with this window by getting the other's opinions of what you put in, what you left out, etc.

---

*Adapted from the ''Balance Sheet'' in *Decision Making* by Irving Janis and Leon Mann Free Press (1977)

BE AWARE AND WARY (Continued)

Foolish Formula: **Treat memory as an enemy.**

Even a good memory can be a handicap. Begin a series of memory exercises by making the following list.

Most Important Life Events: Write below the five most important events in your life.

1. _____
2. _____
3. _____
4. _____
5. _____

One of the problems of writing your own biography is that your mind remembers selectively. Another problem is that most memories only work backward. For example, in the list above, how many important events in your life did you list that have not yet happened? Most people have a hard time thinking forward. Perhaps you did list some future events. The next activity provides practice in future thinking.

Now list the five most important life events in your future.

1. _____
2. _____
3. _____
4. _____
5. _____

Which is easier for you, remembering the past or imaging the future?

☐ Past   ☐ Future

Which do you think you know better, your past or future?

☐ Past   ☐ Future

Most of us have not had much practice in imaging the future. But if we want an ambidextrous memory, we need to work our mind in both directions. The future doesn't exist; it must be invented. It will be invented by someone. You have two choices: invent it or let someone else invent it. The best way to invent a future you want is to practice imaging it.

An Ambidextrous Memory

Your memory may also need practice in working backward, in revising your past. Your past may be out of date; it may need revision. Now look again at your list of important events and review the past events. Pick one past event that is significant to your present. Try to revise your view of it. Look at it from different angles, with new lenses, with hindsight. Try to reinvent your past.

Event: _____

Write down several new views of this event: positive/negative, important/unimportant, how someone else would interpret it/how you might misinterpret it. Use the six thinking hats (objective, emotional, etc.).

New Views: _____

_____

Your memory is an enemy in several ways:

- It remembers selectively
- It usually works only backward
- Its old knowledge becomes out of date
- Its old knowledge blocks new knowing

You not only need an open mind (aware and wary), you also need a multi-directional memory (backward and forward). Be on the watch for insight, forget what you recollect, revise what you remember, image and design what will happen.

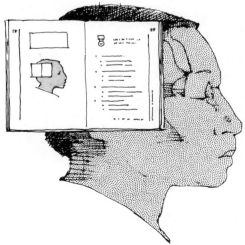

The Case of Susan

Remember Susan who was good at getting the facts. She was good at being aware; she wasn't as good at being wary. To Susan, making her choice of college was merely a matter of collecting all the relevant information.

Susan neglected to be wary of potential misinformation and of what she didn't know before she made her decision. After enrolling in the college of her choice, she found that the college catalog provided some reliable information but not all of the relevant knowledge. Facts she had collected were either no longer true or were not as important as she once thought. Information from alumni was not always "innocent."

Susan discovered that the more she knew about choosing a college, by learning from the experience of choosing one, the more she didn't know. There were many more uncertainties than she realized. Susan became someone who no longer was certain that getting the facts always means having the knowledge.

In what ways are you like Susan? What are your attitudes and skills in the what you know factor of decision making? Check ☑ the following answers that apply to you.

Personal Review

1. Do you think it is possible to be both aware and wary?
   - ☐ yes
   - ☐ no
   - ☐ maybe

2. Do you think it is desirable?
   - ☐ yes
   - ☐ no
   - ☐ maybe

3. Are you best at:
   - ☐ seeing knowledge as power
   - ☐ seeing ignorance as bliss
   - ☐ being balanced

4. Are you best at:
   - ☐ treating memory as an ally
   - ☐ treating memory as an enemy
   - ☐ being balanced

5. Are you best at:
   - ☐ using information
   - ☐ using imagination
   - ☐ being balanced

6. How would you rate your skill in developing creative answers to the "what else" questions?
   - ☐ outstanding
   - ☐ adequate
   - ☐ needs to improve

Summary

Creative decision making using Positive Uncertainty recommends:

- Being aware and wary about what you know

- Recognizing that knowledge is power and ignorance is bliss

- Treating memory as an enemy

- Balancing using information and imagination

Positive Uncertainty requires a paradoxical balance. The more you know, the more you realize you don't know. The key is to accept this uncertainty but not to be paralyzed by it. Not knowing for certain opens the opportunity for new knowledge.

In making decisions, you need to be aware of some things: what you could do, what could happen, and the probability and importance of what could happen. But when knowledge is constantly changing, you also need to be wary of what you know. The same is true of what you don't know.

Information isn't always informative. The skill of being wary helps you deal with the fact that there is no such thing as ''innocent information.'' Daniel Goldbert's first law of expertise explains, ''Never ask the barber if you need a haircut.'' And it is also true that your own advice is ''tainted.''

The balance of being aware and wary requires the ability to learn and unlearn. This paradoxical principle is not new but it is now necessary.

> To attain knowledge, add things every day.
> To attain wisdom, remove things every day.
> Lao-tse in the *Tao Te Ching*

*P*ART III ▪ **PARADOXICAL PRINCIPLE #3:**

BE OBJECTIVE AND OPTIMISTIC
About What You Believe

> *Reality is the leading cause of stress amongst those who are in touch with it.*
> Jane Wagner

Believing is seeing. Quantum physics has taught us that our beliefs are our ''spectacles.'' They cause us to see things a certain way; they show us our reality. Reality is what we take to be true. What we take to be true is what we believe.

This phenomenon has significant implications for your future and how you make decisions. Your decisions partly determine your future, but they also partly reflect what you believe it to be. Your vision of the future may be the most important factor in determining it. Life may really be a self-fulfilling prophecy. If you think you can, you might; if you think you can't, you're right. Everything begins with belief.

We have always known about the power of our beliefs, but the modern age has introduced scientific credibility. Scientific methods try to eliminate the influence of our beliefs from our observations. Rational objectivity, the essence of linear science and of classical decision theory, implies that we should seek a view of reality that is ''undistorted.'' However, quantum physics shows that beliefs are not only impossible to eliminate but desirable to cultivate. A balance between fact and fancy is needed. Being objective is not obsolete, but it is no longer sufficient.

Irrational subjectivity can be advantageous: it can lead you astray or to unrealistic optimism about the future. Unrealistic optimism is part of a healthy mind, which sometimes needs to distort reality in order to adjust to it successfully. If you cannot and should not always be rationally objective, learn to sometimes be unrealistically optimistic.

BE OBJECTIVE AND OPTIMISTIC (Continued)

> *Ambiguous Advice:* **Reality is in the eye of the beholder and the I of the beholder.**

Reality is partly what you see it to be (the eye of the beholder) and partly what you make it to be (the I of the beholder). Therefore, it takes both dreaming and doing. This leads to the biggest paradox of believing is seeing is doing. The motto of the Scientific School of Police in Paris says: "The eye sees in things what it looks for, and it looks for what is already in the mind." But Positive Uncertainty says: "The I does things it believes it can do, and what it believes it can do is what it chooses to believe." What you choose to believe is up to you. It is truly a powerful option. Do you know what you believe?

Metaphor As Method

If your vision and future image are so important, you should know what they are. Knowing your beliefs will be an important tool for planning and creating your future. Knowing, however, involves two parts of your mind: conscious and unconscious, rational and intuitive, cognitive and imagery. Most people are more familiar with one part or the other. Most people are either left- or right-brained. One way to bridge this gap between the two minds, to find out about your future vision or to develop it, is with metaphor.

A metaphor calls a thing something it isn't: "Life is a bowl of cherries." Metaphors are not logical, but they create an image that can challenge what is blindly accepted, allow new links to develop and generate new ways of thinking. Metaphors are a way of understanding a situation you are a part of and helped create. They give you a new language, a more poetic, less scientific language, for discussion of life.

Your life is like a metaphor. Sometimes you can understand it, sometimes you can't. Sometimes it is sad, sometimes funny. Sometimes it just doesn't seem complete, yet at other times it may seem perfect. In many cases it appears that there must be more learning to it; and the more you think about it, the more you understand it.

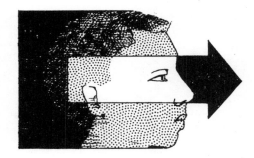

Metaphors of the Future

The following two-part metaphor activity, adapted from Draper Kaufmann, *Teaching The Future*, will help you get acquainted with your future vision. Read the four metaphors and decide which one comes closest to your future vision. Assume this is a multiple-choice, forced-choice decision; you must choose one. It may not be exactly right, but it is better than the others.

Four Metaphors

1. *Roller Coaster*

The future is a great roller coaster. It twists ahead of us in the dark, although we can only see each part as we come to it. We can sometimes see around the bend but the future is fixed and determined. We are locked in our seats and nothing we may know or do will change the course that is laid out for us.

2. *Mighty River*

The future is a mighty river. The great force of history flows along, carrying us with it. Its course can be changed but only by natural disasters, like earthquakes and landslides, or by massive concerted human efforts on a similar scale. However, we are free as individuals to adapt to the course of history, either well or poorly. By looking ahead, we can avoid sandbars and whirlpools and pick the best path through any rapids.

3. *Great Ocean*

The future is a great ocean. There are many possible destinations, and many different paths to each destination. By taking advantage of the main currents of change, keeping a sharp lookout posted, and moving carefully in uncharted waters, a good navigator can get safely to the charted destination, barring a typhoon or other disaster that cannot be predicted or avoided.

4. *Colossal Dice Game*

The future is entirely random, a colossal dice game. Every second things happen that could have happened another way to produce another future. Since everything is chance, all we can do is play the game, pray to the gods of fortune and enjoy what good luck comes our way.

BE OBJECTIVE AND OPTIMISTIC (Continued)

Metaphors of the Future (Continued)

Which of the four metaphors described on page 39 most closely resembles your vision of the future? Check ✍ one.

____ **1.** Roller Coaster   ____ **3.** Great Ocean

____ **2.** Mighty River   ____ **4.** Colossal Dice Game

Why? _____

_____

_____

_____

What didn't you like about the others? _____

_____

_____

Do you think you can control your future? How much do you think you can affect future events?

_____

_____

_____

Your answer may not be well-developed yet because you haven't given it a lot of thought. But your answer is very important to your decision making and often determines what you do. Keep working on your answer; metaphors may be helpful.

Your Personal Metaphor

Now create your own metaphor of the future, or of life if you prefer. What best describes your vision? Try to use something familiar to you: a hobby, favorite thing, activity, or animal—anything. Don't worry about being fancy or poetic.

To me, the future is _____

_____

_____

_____

Keep this metaphor and work with it, expand it, modify it, change it, or get a new one. See if it can't give you some insights into your future vision or to help you expand or change your vision.

Vision Testing

Good vision is important to a good future. Vision means the act or power of seeing, or the act or power of imagination. In a way, the two definitions are the same because we now know that believing is seeing. Some people need to improve their ability to visualize (the act or power of imagination). Others need to improve their ability to revise their visions ("change spectacles").

Your vision (belief system), like your body, automobile, or finances, should have a regular checkup and maintenance plan. The vision in the mind's eye is so important in decision making that it should always be kept in good working condition. Positive Uncertainty suggests regular vision testing. What is the condition of your mind's eye?

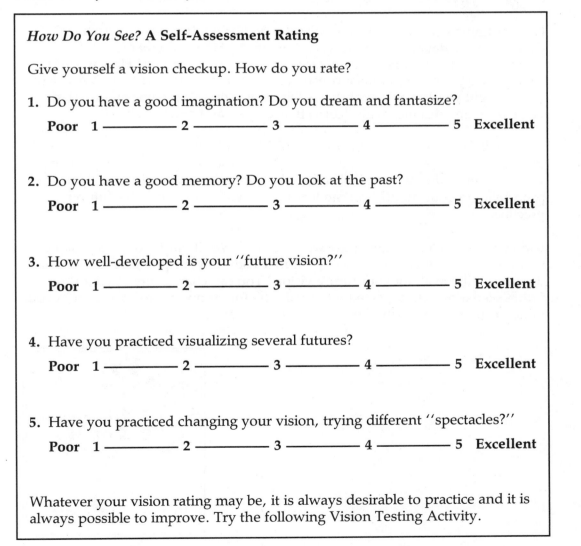

How Do You See? **A Self-Assessment Rating**

Give yourself a vision checkup. How do you rate?

1. Do you have a good imagination? Do you dream and fantasize?

    Poor 1 ———— 2 ———— 3 ———— 4 ———— 5 Excellent

2. Do you have a good memory? Do you look at the past?

    Poor 1 ———— 2 ———— 3 ———— 4 ———— 5 Excellent

3. How well-developed is your "future vision?"

    Poor 1 ———— 2 ———— 3 ———— 4 ———— 5 Excellent

4. Have you practiced visualizing several futures?

    Poor 1 ———— 2 ———— 3 ———— 4 ———— 5 Excellent

5. Have you practiced changing your vision, trying different "spectacles?"

    Poor 1 ———— 2 ———— 3 ———— 4 ———— 5 Excellent

Whatever your vision rating may be, it is always desirable to practice and it is always possible to improve. Try the following Vision Testing Activity.

BE OBJECTIVE AND OPTIMISTIC (Continued)

Future Scenario Scripting

Imagine the future one year from now. Imagine what you will be doing, where, with whom, how, why, etc. For the following three scenarios, experience what it is like, how you feel, act, what you like, and don't like. Take a few moments for each one. Close your eyes and imagine you are really there, one year from now, doing what you are imagining.

1. The probable future: the one you predict will happen

2. The best future: the most desirable one you can imagine

3. The worst future: the most undesirable one you can imagine

Now examine your three visions. Was the probable future easy to visualize? Could you see details clearly or were they fuzzy? How did you feel while experiencing it? Was one year too far away or too near for you? How would you characterize your expectations: conservative, exciting, "far out," etc.? Was what you thought would happen objective? Explain. You can become an expert at visualizing any distance with "corrective lenses" and practice exercises.

Was the best future vision easy or difficult? Was it really the best you can possibly imagine or just the best you could expect? How did you feel while experiencing it? Was your most desirable vision distorted by optimism or pessimism? By unlikely probability in your mind? You can learn to imagine more desirable futures with practice.

Did you have a clear vision of the worst future? Was it harder or easier than the best future? Was your best or worst future closest to your probable future? What does this tell you about your future vision? You can change any of your three future scenarios with repeated rehearsal. The future doesn't exist, except in your mind. You can change the future right behind your eyes.

Foolish Formula: **Treat Beliefs as Prophecy**

> *The ultimate function of prophecy is not to tell the future but to make it.*
> W. W. Wagar

The belief system is not just a state of mind. It is a physiological reality. Your positive or negative beliefs can actually increase or decrease your immune cells, dilate or constrict your capillaries, and decrease or increase your pulse rate. This has been proven by research on the placebo effect and other scientific phenomena, thus demonstrating how beliefs become biology.

Shelly Taylor's research in *Positive Illusions* shows that three adaptive misconceptions can be positive illusions that create self-fulfilling prophecies. It appears that people are mentally healthy because of certain positive illusions about themselves and their environment. These positive illusions enable one to do something and to manage negative feedback. The three adaptive misconceptions:

- Unrealistic optimism for the future

- Exaggerated perceptions of personal control

- Unrealistically positive view of self

Taylor's findings contradict many psychologists' and counseling professionals' view that a primary criterion of mental health is an accurate perception of self, the present reality, and the probable future. But this criterion is clearly changing. Another paradox is recognized: illusions can be a sign of pathology, or they can make life worth living. What we now must accept is that denial (refusing to face the facts) and illusion (false beliefs about reality) have their usefulness in coping and may sometimes be the healthiest strategies in certain situations.

There is probably nothing more powerful, and more empowering, than what you believe about yourself and your future. Optimism is a belief and it can be learned. There is now scientific evidence that optimism is vitally important in improving mental and physical health, overcoming defeat, and promoting achievement.

BE OBJECTIVE AND OPTIMISTIC (Continued)

Become Good At Dreaming

Creating your future requires that you dream it and do it. If you could improve your dreaming you could improve your doing. Dreaming is not a left-brain activity; therefore, it gets neglected. However, there actually are some good reasons for learning to become good at dreaming.

Dreams do come true, even impossible dreams. Maybe if we dreamed more impossible dreams, we'd have more coming true. Maybe if we practiced dreaming more, we'd have more impossible dreams.

Answer the following questions: Yes, No, or Maybe.

    ____ **1.** Is it unwise to believe impossible things?

    ____ **2.** Is it silly to practice doing it?

    ____ **3.** Is it possible to know which things are impossible?

Is it possible to run a mile in less than four minutes? Was it once impossible? Is it possible for someone to walk on the moon? Was it once impossible? ''Anything one man can imagine, other men can make real.'' (Jules Verne) How do we know which things are impossible? We don't, as one of Murphy's Laws points out: ''Some things are impossible to know, but it is impossible to know these things.''

Like the problem with our one-way memory, which works best backward, our one-way believing is usually better at visualizing fear than fantasy. Most people dread precisely but dream vaguely. Using the impossible dreaming exercise on the next page, practice dreaming precisely, about ''impossible'' futures, including all the wonderful specific details.

Impossible Dreaming Exercise

Practice believing some impossible things by visualizing a fantasy dream come true. Imagine you are living the "best future scenario" from the last exercise (page 42). Use all the adaptive misconceptions and positive illusions you can think of. Dream precisely, make it fantastic. Take a few moments, close your eyes, enjoy.

It would help if you could tell someone your dream or say it out loud to yourself. Were you precise? Did you experience it? Did you enjoy it? Could you make it better the next time? Could you make it an "impossible" scenario next time? You could, if you practice.

Some people, when creating a future scenario, cannot imagine a highly desirable future for themselves. They cannot see themselves as part of a positive future. That comes from being "too good" at being objective. It comes from many negative previous experiences; it comes from being taught not to. It comes from lack of practice; it comes from many factors. But it *can* be overcome.

What would happen if people learned to dream impossible (optimistic) dreams more often? Or become skilled at imagining desirable future scenarios? Running a mile in less than four minutes requires two things: believing you can do it and doing it. The first may be just as important as the second. What if life really is a self-fulfilling prophecy?

Vision testing in positive uncertainty is a process for examining and educating the eye of the beholder. Vision testing is the opposite of reality testing. Most of us have a lot of practice testing reality, "being realistic," but not as much experience with "wishful thinking," being optimistic. The examining and correctional activities of positive uncertainty will help the decision maker to explore the beliefs and visions in the mind's eye and will assist in developing at least a balance between optimism and objectivity about the future. But how do you find the right balance between "unrealistic optimism" and "impossible objectivity?"

The problem, of course, is that the two are intimately related. Being optimistic about what might happen, can change what does happen. Being positive and confident in what you are trying to accomplish lets you relax and, paradoxically, concentrate. The decision maker, who feels confident, like the baseball team, will relax, and probably be more successful.

The Case of Dave

Remember Dave who was realistic about his future, with both feet on the ground. He wasn't going to be caught with foolish expectations. Dave had his ''head on straight.'' He wouldn't let false hope or future fantasies distract him.

What Dave didn't realize was that reality was in the eye of the beholder. And so was his hope for the future. When Dave was faced with ''a new reality'' of moving to a new location with a new beginning for him, he couldn't imagine a happy ending. After moving to another part of the country Dave discovered that he was right, he didn't experience a happy ending. Life was, indeed, a self-fulfilling prophecy.

We don't know, of course, what would have happened if Dave had a different belief about his move. We do know, however, that what he did about his future move would have been different. Dave's image of his future is one of the most important factors in determining it. Even unrealistic optimism about the future is more empowering than rational objectivity.

In what ways are you like Dave? What are the attitudes and skills in the what you believe factor of decision making? Check the following answers that apply to you.

Personal Review

1. Do you think it is possible to be both objective and optimistic?
   - ☐ yes
   - ☐ no
   - ☐ maybe

2. Do you think it is desirable?
   - ☐ yes
   - ☐ no
   - ☐ maybe

3. Are you best at acknowledging that reality is:
   - ☐ in the eye of the beholder (what you see)
   - ☐ in the I of the beholder (what you do)
   - ☐ being balanced

4. Are you best at:
   - ☐ treating beliefs as self-deceptive
   - ☐ treating beliefs as prophecy
   - ☐ being balanced

5. Are you best at:
   - ☐ reality testing
   - ☐ wishful thinking
   - ☐ being balanced

6. How would you rate your skill of ''vision testing'' using metaphor and scenario scripting?
   - ☐ outstanding
   - ☐ adequate
   - ☐ needs to improve

Summary

Creative decision making using Positive Uncertainty recommends:

- Being objective and optimistic
- Noticing that reality is in the eye of the beholder and the I of the beholder
- Treating beliefs as prophecy
- Balancing reality testing with wishful thinking

The what you believe principle may be the most powerful one of all. Your beliefs not only partly determine what you do, they also partly determine what you want and know. Rigid beliefs make you rigid in decision making. When you change your beliefs you change your spectacles: you change what you want, know, see, and do. Revising your beliefs and your vision of the future could be a useful skill to develop for navigating the rapids of a turbulent river.

People do not live life totally rationally or objectively. One cannot dance with the left brain. But people can learn how to use a balance of the rational and intuitive, the objective and subjective in making choices about what to do. However, the role of what you believe cannot be underestimated.

> *Reality is illusion, and only illusion is real.*
> Don Quixote

PART IV ▪ PARADOXICAL PRINCIPLE #4:

BE PRACTICAL AND MAGICAL
About What You Do

> *Don't do what you shouldn't unless there is a very good reason why you should.*
> Ashleigh Brilliant

Paradoxical Principle #4 is about what you do to decide what to do. It's about what methods, rules, or procedures you use to make decisions.

Of course, rule books and authoritative procedures will tell you how you should decide. Rules for living are taught in every classroom from kindergarten to college. People love rules that tell them what to do, and they hate them. It's another paradox of life. We want to be captain of our ship, but we also want a pilot's manual. People crave but fear autonomy—taking responsibility for making the decisions which give shape to one's life. It's our beloved freedom of choice. People who fear making decisions will use many techniques, often unconsciously, to avoid it. However, one cannot avoid making decisions.

Imagine this scenario: the burned-out executive has just finished an extensive physical examination and is listening to the physician's prescription for recovery. What she hears is: ''I recommend you give up drinking, smoking and decision making.'' Giving up drinking and smoking is difficult but possible because other people have done it. Nobody has been able to give up decision making because even not to decide is to decide. The best prescription for a healthy decision maker is not to give up decision making but to give up the fear and stress usually associated with it. This chapter might be entitled, ''The Joy of Deciding.''

Positive Uncertainty's prescription for putting joy into deciding is: be practical and magical about what you do to decide. Practical means businesslike, sensible, reasonable, and down to earth—the rational side of your mind. Magical means mysterious, delightful, effortless, and pie in the sky—the intuitive side. This principle could be called a decision rule, but it isn't the authoritative and precise kind of rule people love and hate. In fact, it's rather ambiguous. But by now you realize that ambiguity is the Positive Uncertainty approach.

BE PRACTICAL AND MAGICAL (Continued)

Positive Uncertainty's approach must be ambiguous to accommodate the paradoxes of craving and dreading autonomy and loving and hating rules. It involves using some decision rules, making some rules, and breaking some rules. What you do will depend on many things, including what you want, know, and believe. But it shouldn't depend on rigid decision rules. You shouldn't become a prisoner of your procedures.

Everyone has decision procedures, rules, or methods. All methods seem to fall into one of the following categories (or some combination): rational, intuitive, traditional. Most rational rules go something like this: define objectives, analyze alternatives, predict consequences, select the best alternative. Intuitive and traditional methods are highly idiosyncratic. Until recently, rational rules were the prototype of good decision making. Although the rational process was preached as conventional wisdom, it was not commonly practiced. What most people do to decide is private, personal, and unconventional.

Private decision rules often escape awareness. These rules start out as guidelines and end up as straight jackets. In fact, rules often become habits that are too weak to be felt until they are too strong to be broken. Decision makers can help themselves by checking their unnoticed decision habits. Principle #4 does not intend to prescribe a better rule for deciding what to do. It encourages decision makers to develop a repertoire of rational/intuitive/traditional methods, a comfort with such an alliance, an awareness of one's responsibility of choice, and a set of balanced skills for deciding what to do to decide.

Try the following Positive Uncertainty habit-hunting exercise for finding your decision methods that may have become unnoticed habits. This is often difficult to do because sometimes we really don't know how we decide and because the way we think we should decide and the way we do decide are often different.

Imagine you are being interviewed by yourself and you really want to find out what you do to decide. You use some decision rules, even though you may not be sure what they are. You are trying to uncover your habit pattern. This is a self-directed search for clues to your decision methods. It is a habit hunting expedition; it is not a test.

If you have difficulty, concentrate on (or start with) question 4 and use several examples.

Habit Hunting: Look for the methods (habits) you use in making your decisions.

1. Describe several standard operating decision rules as you know them, the ones you were taught or have learned or developed. If you have difficulty, read the methods menu on the next page.

   _____

   _____

   _____

   _____

2. What do you believe is the correct way to decide?

   _____

   _____

3. What is your most common way to decide?

   _____

   _____

4. Describe the way you make specific decisions. Give two examples.

   Decision example one: _____

   • How did you decide that? What decision rule did you use?

   • Why did you decide that way?

   • Describe the way others might have decided in this example.

   Decision example two: _____

   • How did you decide that? What decision rule did you use?

   • Why did you decide that way?

   • Describe the way others might have decided in this example.

Make habit hunting a continuous process in order to be always aware of your decision rules and to be able to expand them.

BE PRACTICAL AND MAGICAL (Continued)

A Methods Menu

Most people claim to use the rational decision method: define objectives, analyze alternatives, predict consequences, and choose the best alternative (the one with the highest expected value, highest probability and desirability). Following are some examples of other decision methods.

Safe: Choose the alternative with the least risk.

Wish: Choose the alternative that could lead to the best outcome, regardless of the risk. ''Go for it.''

Escape: Choose the alternative that is most likely to avoid the worst possible outcome. Escape catastrophe.

Impulsive: Choose by the seat of your pants—leap before you look.

Delaying: Choose to procrastinate or postpone—''Cross that bridge later.''

Fatalistic: Leave it up to fate to decide—''It's in the cards.''

Compliant: Let someone else decide—''Whatever you say.''

Idiosyncratic Examples: Because of my faith or the Holy Scriptures—

''Choose the path less chosen.''

''Do what God would do.''

''Choose the first one'' ''...the last one'' ''...the cheapest one.''

''Choose the easiest one'' ''...the hardest one.''

''Choose the same one I did last time.''

''Do what feels right.''

''Do what my wife (husband, boss, etc.) would do.''

''Add up the pros and cons and decide.''

''Do what others expect.''

''Randomly decide and forget it.''

Add other examples that you know about:

_____

_____

_____

_____

The What You Do Principle

The what you do principle, although the culmination of the decision-making process, is interconnected with the other three basic principles of Positive Uncertainty. The four basic principles cannot be separated in practice as we have done in writing about them.

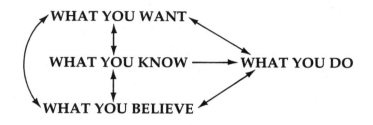

The interconnectedness of these four decision factors makes it impossible to look at only one factor at a time; you cannot separate *what* you do from *looking* at what you do. For example, the minute you decide that what you do makes a difference, it will make a difference in what you do.

To be practical and magical is to be interconnected, to be whole-brained. We need to learn to use all of our creative powers when deciding what to do. We need to learn to use both sides of our brain as if they were partners, because they are. We need to be playful, not fearful when deciding. We need to learn to play with the limitations of our logic and to play with the boundlessness of our intuition. That's being practical and magical.

> The practical side plays *within* boundaries.

> The magical side plays *with* boundaries.

Although the concept of left and right brain is overused and oversimplified, it will be helpful while promoting a ''whole-brained'' approach to decision making. Western thinking is so committed to left-brain logic that it is difficult for some people to seriously consider other approaches to making important decisions about their life. Imagine trying to sell the left brain the idea ''Leap before you look.'' It doesn't make sense to the rational mind. What would the whole-brained mind do about looking and leaping as an approach to living?

Perhaps the following two different philosophical views will help illustrate the point:

> *The unexamined life is not worth living.* Socrates
>
> *The unlived life is not worth examining.* Max Learner

BE PRACTICAL AND MAGICAL (Continued)

Using A Wholebrain Approach

It would be nice if we didn't have to choose between an unlived life and an unexamined one. Most of us, of course, believe a little bit of both. That's wholebrained thinking.

Another strength of the wholebrain is its ability to work like a computer and not to work like a computer. The computer does not know how to be ambiguous but our mind does. We need to learn how to make better use of our major strength. Our whole brain seems to be perfectly designed for explicitness and clarity and for ambiguity and uncertainty.

There seems to be no invention, no matter how sophisticated, that can equal the power, flexibility, and user-friendliness of the whole human mind. We all possess the world's finest multisensory decision-making machine right in our heads. All we have to do is to learn how to use it.

How good are you at using both sides of your brain? The following exercise is a way to examine how you look at life. Using the Fuzrate technique will allow you to be a little fuzzy in your rating, since you may be a little fuzzy in your appraisal.

Whole Brain Appraisal

Where are you on the left-right brain continuum? Rate yourself. Use the fuzrate technique (see page 19):

1. In using decision rules, do you usually...
   Play within boundaries ——+—+—+—+—+—+—+—+—+—+— Play with boundaries.

2. In making choices, do you usually...
   Look before you leap ——+—+—+—+—+—+—+—+—+—+— Leap before you look.

3. In your philosophy of life, do you usually...
   Value the examined life ——+—+—+—+—+—+—+—+—+—+— Value the lived life.

4. In working with information, do you usually...
   Prefer precise data ——+—+—+—+—+—+—+—+—+—+— Prefer sloppy data.

5. In deciding what to do, do you usually...
   Rely on your left brain ——+—+—+—+—+—+—+—+—+—+— Rely on your right brain.

Your answers may give you some idea about where you are on the practical—magical decision-making continuum. Some ambiguous advice and a foolish formula may cause you to move your position.

> *Ambiguous Advice:* **Learn to plan and plan to learn.**

We already know that planning for the future may be unfeasible because the future is unpredictable and people are irrational. In Part IV you should learn to plan the future. This recommendation makes sense only if you add, ''and plan to learn.'' Like the other ambiguous advice of Positive Uncertainty, learn to plan and plan to learn has two sides, and it takes both sides to make the whole.

When it comes to the future, there are three kinds of people:

- Those who make it happen
- Those who watch it happen
- Those who wonder what happened

What kind of person you are (what you decide to do about your future) is what this book is all about. Decision making can be used to cause change or to adapt to change. It can be used to predict the future and prepare for what is predicted. Or it can be used to imagine the future and create the future that is imagined. You can decide to do either or you can decide to do both. But if you decide to do nothing, you'll end up wondering what happened.

The future doesn't exist; it must be invented and constructed. You have two choices, make the future happen or watch it happen. Positive Uncertainty suggests that decision makers develop a balance between doing and watching. It's a balance between learning to plan (setting goals, devising strategies, predicting outcomes) and planning to learn (expecting change, visualizing change, causing change). Two kinds of decision-making skills are needed.

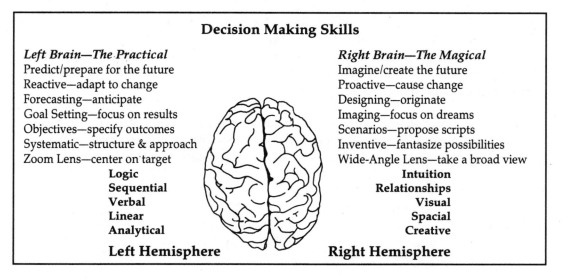

Decision Making Skills

Left Brain—The Practical	*Right Brain—The Magical*
Predict/prepare for the future	Imagine/create the future
Reactive—adapt to change	Proactive—cause change
Forecasting—anticipate	Designing—originate
Goal Setting—focus on results	Imaging—focus on dreams
Objectives—specify outcomes	Scenarios—propose scripts
Systematic—structure & approach	Inventive—fantasize possibilities
Zoom Lens—center on target	Wide-Angle Lens—take a broad view

Logic	Intuition
Sequential	Relationships
Verbal	Visual
Linear	Spacial
Analytical	Creative

Left Hemisphere **Right Hemisphere**

Using A Wholebrain Approach (Continued)

Since you apparently have more than one brain, why not use the whole? Think of the advantage of viewing the future with both a wide-angle lens and a zoom lens.

Review the left-brain/right-brain skills and indicate your strengths and weaknesses on the following continuum, once again using the fuzrate scale.

Decision-Making Skills

Left Brain—Practical	Right Brain—The Magical
Predict/Prepare	Imagine/Create
Reactive	Proactive
Forecasting	Designing
Goal Setting	Imaging
Objectives	Scenarios
Systematic	Inventive
Zoom Lens	Wide-Angle Lens

If you are like most decision makers, you have developed some of both kinds of decision skills but don't have a balanced repertoire. Or you may be the kind who decides one way and pretends to decide another. Becoming a whole-brained, creative decision maker does not mean abandoning rational decision skills or the left brain, but it does mean giving equal credibility and involvement to the right side. Some people, of course, will need to become balanced by including more of the practical side of their whole brain approach.

Just as your brain has two sides, so does creativity. To be creative is to be different, uncommon, inventive. Creativity causes change. If you do something differently, change results. But creativity is also needed to respond successfully to change. If your environment changes, you need to respond differently. Creativity is uncertain. So is change.

Change and creativity are both associated with risk, and both cause the fear, anxiety, and disapproval associated with newness. But they also cause joy, excitement, and approval. We want change and creativity, and we also want to avoid them.

To be practical and magical, therefore, lets you have it both ways. If we never do anything differently, if we always follow the rules, we can't be sure of decreasing the uncertainty and risks, but we probably will decrease the joy and excitement.

> *Foolish Formula:* **Treat intuition as real.**

This foolish formula is the key to creative decision making. Intuition is called, among other things, insight, guesswork, sixth sense, hunch, precognition, or direct knowing without evident rational thought. Intuition is sometimes thought of as an excuse for doing something we can't otherwise justify or for refusing to follow the logic of our own beliefs. Treating intuition as real, even though we can't explain it scientifically, permits us to see some possible actions that are outside our present scheme for explaining or justifying behavior.

Using intuition is like improvisation. Conventional decision-making strategies emphasize hard data, facts that can be analyzed. However, hard data analyzes the past, since anything that can be measured or analyzed has already happened. Relying too heavily on this kind of input can deny the intuitive mind the kind of raw material it relies upon. Whole brained decision makers will sometimes want to improvise.

You can practice developing your own magical decision style, learning to improvise. Since other things can be disguised as intuition, find out if it is real, and treat it that way, with all the rights and privileges granted to reason and logic. Try the following personal interrogation activity whenever you run into what you think is intuition.

Is It Really Intuition? A Personal Interrogation.

Ask yourself these questions whenever you're unsure if your improvisation is really intuition.*

Is it intuition or is it . . .

1. *Fear of uncertainty?* Does it provide you relief from indecision or ambiguity?
2. *Desire?* Is it wishful thinking, a powerful hope, you want strongly to believe?
3. *Impulsiveness?* Is it reactive, out-of-control behavior?
4. *Emotion?* Did you ''intuit'' from anger, intimidation, a need to feel victimized?
5. *Intellectual laziness?* Is it justification for the easy way out?
6. *Image-making?* Is it a need to appear decisive, confident, self-assured?
7. *Rebelliousness?* Do you need to be different, fight authority, avoid knuckling under?

The personal interrogation appears to be a contradiction since it asks you to analyze intuition. But it is really an example of using both sides of the brain, whole-brained thinking. Remember the fine line between positive illusions and self-deception discussed in Part III, ''What You Believe.'' Learning to trust your intuition is part of the paradox of being objective and optimistic.

*Adapted from Goldberg, *The Intuitive Edge*

BE PRACTICAL AND MAGICAL (Continued)

Developing Your Practical/Magical Decision-Making Style

To become a better whole brained decision maker you can do at least three things.

- Bring unconscious decision methods and habits into awareness. You can begin to know the decision procedures you use by continuing to work on the habit hunting exercise. Bringing unconscious habits, thoughts, and intuition into creative awareness leads to effective decision making. By knowing what you do, not what you pretend to do, you can decide to do what you want to do. You can avoid becoming a prisoner of your procedures. You become creative and flexible.

- Strive to develop a balance between practical and magical methods. Continue to assess your status with the whole-brain appraisal and the decision-making skills continuum or other devices. Use these appraisals to strengthen your weak areas and achieve more balance.

- Learn to master paradox. Our changing society requires that we learn to love change, not just adjust to it. In a time of unprecedented change, uncertainty and chaos, positive uncertainty recommends mastering the four paradoxical principles for thriving on the chaos.

A paradox seems contradictory, even absurd, but may actually be true. To master paradox, tomorrow's decision makers must become comfortable with contradiction and absurdity. They must be flexible, wary, optimistic, and magical. They also must be focused, aware, objective, and practical. They will learn to succeed more by failing more; they will learn to make rules and to break rules; they will learn to respond creatively to change and to create change; and they will learn to plan and plan to learn.

Practical and Magical Put Together

To help you in developing your own balanced, creative decision style, the following decision tree model is one approach to using both the rational and intuitive when deciding what to do. Your approach may be something like this, a variation, a combination of certain parts, something quite different, or all of the above.

In Part II, ''Be Aware and Wary,'' we said that decision making has three parts: Actions, Outcomes, and the Uncertainty between actions and outcomes. The uncertainty involves the desirability of the outcomes and their probability. Choosing, therefore, requires one to look at:

1. Options, alternatives.
   Possible actions you could take. What you could do.

2. Outcomes, consequences.
   Possible results of your actions. What could happen.

3. Desirability of outcome.
   Personal preferences. How much you will value what happens.

4. Probability of outcomes.
   The chance of a consequence happening. Likelihood of results.

When you make a choice of what to do, you can never know what the outcome will be or how you will respond. You can't be sure what will happen as a result of what you decide to do. You can't be sure how much you will really like or dislike what happens until it happens. Studying the facts and reviewing scientific data will help you with calculations and predictions. But studying your feelings and tuning-in to your hunches can also help you with imagination and prophecy. However, the uncertainty cannot be eliminated.

DECISION TREE IMAGERY

One way to assimilate the practical and magical is to visualize a decision tree. Imagine a picture of your decision with the four decision parts listed above. You can, of course, draw the picture and fill in the blanks for a particular decision, using many decision trees and branches for all the options and outcomes. However, if you can plant such a decision tree imagery in your mind's eye, it can be useful in developing your repertoire of decision strategies for big or small decisions.

This decision tree model is borrowed from the highly rational decision strategies and is intended to help decision makers think through the uncertainties using both rational and intuitive processes and make their own decision as to how to decide. No attempt will be made to describe the difficult rational process of estimating the combined value of probability and desirability.

Decision Tree Imagery

OPTIONS	**OUTCOMES**	**DESIRABILITY**	**PROBABILITY**
Possible Actions	Possible Results	Preferences	Likelihood
	One Outcome	Low ──┼┼┼── High	Low ──┼┼┼── High
One Option ─<			
	Another Outcome	Low ──┼┼┼── High	Low ──┼┼┼── High

This gives you a visual starting point. Using this visual model, you can bounce between the rational and intuitive methods and decide what to do when you feel ready or when you must. The following steps are not intended to be prescriptive but to give you a basis to develop your own idiosyncratic whole brained decision style. The decision tree imagery example can be used with the Ponder Your Resignation exercise in Part II to illustrate its possibilities; you might want to pick a real decision you have already made or are about to make and use it as an illustration.

As you use this visual model, remember to ask "What else could I do?" and "What else could happen?" You might be forgetting other important options and outcomes. However, for this exercise, try to narrow your decison to a yes/no an either/or choice; for example, "quit my job or stay." Next, think of one very desirable and one very undesirable outcome. Finally, put in your best estimate or probability for each. These three steps are filled in for the first option as an illustration below.

Decision Tree Imagery Illustration

OPTIONS	OUTCOMES	DESIRABILITY	PROBABILITY
Possible Actions	Possible Results	Preferences	Likelihood

Quit
- **Get better job**   Low —+++— High   Low —+++— High
- **Can't find work**   Low —+++— High   Low —+++— High

Stay
- **Learn to like it**   Low —+++— High   Low —+++— High
- **Things get worse**   Low —+++— High   Low —+++— High

Of course, more than two possible outcomes exist. To help you think of others superimpose the outcomes window from Part II into your imagery.

OPTIONS	OUTCOMES	DESIRABILITY	PROBABILITY
Possible Actions	Possible Results	Preferences	Likelihood

Quit job
- to self
- to others

POSITIVE	NEGATIVE
OUTCOMES	

The diagrams should help you look at the information you are arranging and rearranging in your "two minds" and help you decide on how to make the choice. Do you have the facts? Is what you want distorting the facts? Will what you believe make a difference in the outcome? What do your hunches say? Can you trust your intuition?

Review your decision tree imagery. Where did you get that probability estimate? Is that outcome really that desirable? Undesirable? The visual model helps you make a map of your decision process to help you make up your mind. Sometimes you may want to be very logical, collecting factual data. Other times you may not be able to or want to. Many times it will be a combination, your combination.

BE PRACTICAL AND MAGICAL (Continued)

The Internal Debate Dialogue

One way to select the right combination is with the internal debate dialogue. Imagine you are facing the ''quit job or stay'' decision or pick a real two-option decision you have already made or will make soon. Have a dialog with yourself about the two options using each side of the brain:

> **Left side** = Rational/practical: Businesslike, sensible, and reasonable

> **Right side** = Intuitive/magical: Playful, mysterious, and illogical.

Decision: _____

Option: _____

In the boxes below, first list everything you can think of in support of one option, using each side of the brain. Then list the people who would support each side. You might want to repeat this process with the second option.

Use the internal dialog to debate with yourself, using arguments that are rational and intuitive. Notice how you feel about each argument. This tells you something. Also notice who is on each side. What kind of people are they? Does their opinion matter? Would you like to be more like them? What does their position tell you?

The Internal Debate Dialogue

Left: Rational/Practical	Right: Intuitive/Magical
People who would support this side.	**People who would support this side.**

Decisions aren't made by information or analytical models but by people. More information and more analysis isn't always the answer. Sometimes you have to make a choice somewhere between rational and intuitive. Make it with Positive Uncertainty.

The Case of Alan

Remember Alan who was always practical. He was businesslike and methodical in how he made his decisions. He was good at using his head but not his heart, good at the scientific approach but not the gut-feeling approach.

Alan rejected intuition as improper for the important business and financial decisions in his life. He conducted market research and consumer surveys, studied the latest trends in society, predicted the future of products before development, and analyzed the history of stocks before investing.

Alan discovered that some business and investment hunches paid off for friends and competitors. He also found that his research and predictions sometimes missed the mark. New trends occurred before they could be studied. Sometimes his feelings about what he should do were better than his scientific evidence.

In what ways are you like Alan? What are your attitudes and skills in the what you do factor of decision making? Check ☑ the following answers that apply to you.

Personal Review

1. Do you think it is possible to be both practical and magical?
   ☐ yes
   ☐ no
   ☐ maybe

2. Do you think it is desirable?
   ☐ yes
   ☐ no
   ☐ maybe

3. Are you best at:
   ☐ learning to plan
   ☐ planning to learn
   ☐ being balanced

4. Are you best at:
   ☐ treating intuition as illusory
   ☐ treating intuition as real
   ☐ being balanced

5. Are you best at:
   ☐ responding to change
   ☐ causing change
   ☐ being balanced

6. How would you rate your skill of using wholebrainness
   ☐ outstanding
   ☐ adequate
   ☐ needs to improve

Summary

Positive Uncertainty won't provide you a set of rigid rules for making decisions. In fact, creative decision making requires breaking some rules and making up some rules as you go along. Therefore, what you do to decide is left up to you, without a formula or a faithful, inflexible set of directions. However, creative decision making using Positive Uncertainty recommends:

- Being practical and magical about what you do to decide
- Learning to plan and plan to learn
- Treating intuition as real
- Balancing responding to change and causing change.

What you do is so interconnected with what you want, know and believe that it is hard to talk about it separately. But we did it in this chapter. What you do is the methods, procedures, and rules used in deciding what to decide. Positive Uncertainty does not recommend a set of standardized rules because they don't leave much room for creative ideas. Positive Uncertainty presents guidelines and encourages the growing of new ideas.

The paradoxical principle suggests:

> Habit Hunting—look for the routine methods you use.
> Methods Menu—develop a repertoire of decision methods.
> Wholebrain Appraisal—assess your wholebrainness.
> Decision-Making Skills Continuum—balance practical and magical.
> Personal Interrogation—ask questions to expose disguised intuition.
> Decision Tree Imagery—make decisions when "ready."
> Internal Debate Dialog—debate the rational/intuitive.

In the end, everyone decides for themselves, using whatever method they choose. Using positive uncertainty for creative decision making means choosing from many possible methods and being flexible and versatile in your choices. And being flexible in our choices means we can adapt to change and lead fuller, richer lives.

> *Whenever I have a choice between two evils,*
> *I always choose the one I haven't tried before.*
>
> Mae West

A Summary of Positive Uncertainty
COMMANDMENTS OF CHOICE

The Commandments of Choice are a summary of Positive Uncertainty for the purpose of providing guidance in the application of its 2 x 4 approach to decision making and future planning. In order to make them easy to remember and credible they will be intentionally short and fuzzy.

Short because we have learned that the human mind can remember a maximum of seven things at one time. How many people do you know who can remember all of the Ten Commandments? There will be just four commandments, in order to accommodate even the less than maximum mind.

And fuzzy because Pratt's Law of Understanding tells us that ''If something is easy to understand, no one will believe it is true.'' For example, how many people do you know who act as if they believe in the Golden Rule? The Four Commandments will strive to be a little ambiguous, partly paradoxical, and slightly obscure so people will be more likely to remember them, believe them, and act on them.

Positive Uncertainty is a 2×4 approach to making decisions when you don't know what the future will be. It includes two attitudes: (1) accept uncertainty, and (2) be positive about it. It includes four factors: (1) what you want, (2) what you know, (3) what you believe, and (4) what you do. The Four Commandments of Choice parallel the four factors and employ the two attitudes.

THE FOUR COMMANDMENTS

1 **Thou shall not worship false goals.**

Being sure of what you want and finding out it isn't has always been a nuisance for decision makers. The usual solution, trying harder to be sure, only makes the problem worse. Sometimes getting what you want is worse than not getting it.

The best way to avoid worshipping false goals is not to *worship* any goals. Treat goals as hypotheses. Know what you want but don't be sure. The paradox of this commandment is that although you don't want to worship false goals you don't want to stop setting goals. The process of goal-setting is more important than the goal. Decision making should be as much a process for discovering goals as for achieving them. ''Life is a journey not a destination.''

- Getting what you want requires more than wanting. It requires dreaming and doing, dreaming and doing, dreaming and doing.
- Goals should guide you, not govern you.
- Be focused and be flexible.

The Four Commandments (Continued)

2 Covet thy neighbor's advice.

What you know is usually less than what you don't know. That's reality even in a so-called "Knowledge Society." And if reality is in the eye of the beholder, you should make sure that your reality isn't the only reality you know. "Nothing is more dangerous than an idea when it is the only one you have." (Emile Chartier)

Therefore, get a second and third opinion, *your* second and third opinion, your neighbors, your friend's, your enemy's. And remember, it is harder to profit from advice than it is to give it. Information is food for thought, not thought itself. You won't be starving for knowledge if you use information as food for thought. Thinking that you may not know keeps you open-minded.

The paradox of this commandment is that the more you know, the more you realize you don't know, and yet you can still make decisions and learn. Knowledge is power and ignorance is bliss.

- The basis of most new ideas comes from borrowing, adding, combining, or modifying old ones.

- Information-rich is not know-how wealthy.

- Be aware and be wary.

3 Thou shall sometimes commit credulity.

Credulity is an undue readiness to believe what you want to believe, a tendency toward self-deception, "wishful thinking," "blind faith." The paradox of this commandment is that sometimes these "illusions" are good personal mental health, good planning strategy. It is wise, sometimes, to do some deliberate doubting, to have the courage to challenge your convictions. This helps avoid "unwise self-deception." But it is also wise, sometimes, to do some healthy hoping, to engage in "wise self-deception."

"The eye sees in things what it looks for, and it looks for what is already in the mind." Is that "unwise self-deception?" On the other hand, the "I" does things it believes it can do, and what it believes it can do is what it chooses to believe. Is that "wise self-deception?")

- What you believe your future to be, partly determines what it will be.

- Do not believe in miracles—rely on them. (Finagle's Rule, from Murphy)

- Be objective and be optimistic.

4 Honor thy right and left brain.

Left and right brain are metaphors for rational and intuitive minds. The two, of course, cannot be separated, but the important point is to be good at using both. Two heads are better than one. Your mind and making it up cannot be separated. In fact, your mind and reality cannot be separated.

Being good at using both sides of the brain will require tossing out some old decision dogma. For example, by all means be rational, seek certainty, strive to be consistent, and purpose before action may not always be the best policies. That's the practical, left-brain approach, in the sense of being only businesslike, sensible, reasonable, and logical. But a magical right-brain approach is now also required. Today decision makers need a sense of being creative, risky, inconsistent, idealistic, and instinctive.

- Be rational, unless there is a good reason not to be.

- Take an occasional wild goose chase. That's what wild geese are for.

- Be practical and be magical.

These Commandments are guidelines to guide you, not fences to confine you. Positive Uncertainty's 2×4 approach is a set of potential whole brained procedures for consideration by decision makers. But don't become a prisoner of your procedures. Don't become a tool of your rules. Just do it.

The minute you make up your mind that what you do makes a difference, it will make a difference in what you do.

EPILOGUE

Is Positive Uncertainty Valid?

> *It is by logic that we prove. It is by intuition that we discover.*
> Henri Poincare

Does Positive Uncertainty really work? It is impossible to scientifically test the validity of the principles of Positive Uncertainty or to prove which decision method is best. If the scientific method can't prove the validity of Positive Uncertainty, what can? The answer, of course, is hindsight. Hindsight works. One of Murphy's advanced laws explains: "Hindsight is an exact science."

By using hindsight you can learn from your decisions. Instead of using the inexact scientific method to *prove* the power of Positive Uncertainty, you can use the exact science of hindsight to *improve* the power of Positive Uncertainty. The objective becomes to learn rather than to confirm. After all, experience is the best teacher. But experience is also the hardest teacher—because she gives the test first and the lesson afterwards.

This leads to Positive Uncertainty's only law: "If at first you don't succeed, you're about average." Or to paraphrase Ohm's Law: "For every bad choice, there is an equal and opposite rejoice." Being able to learn from experience is the most powerful, paradoxical decision-making skill. "There is only one thing more powerful than learning from experience and that is not learning from experience." (Archibald MacLeish) Or as Ziggy points out: "Good judgment comes from experience. And experience comes from poor judgment."

Experience is what you get when you don't get what you want. But if learning is your objective, then you always get what you want. Think of learning as discovering the results of experience. Let life be a lesson to you. "Everyone is a teacher, every experience is a lesson, every relationship a course of study." (Marilyn Ferguson)

So when you are uncertain about your future and have to make up your mind, remember that Positive Uncertainty:

- makes sense even though it isn't scientific,

- helps you learn, even though you make mistakes,

- provides empowerment, even though it doesn't produce proof.

The best way to predict the future is to create it. This book recommends that you create it with Positive Uncertainty.

REFERENCES

Ackoff, Russell, *Redesigning The Future,* New York: Wiley, 1974

de Bono, Edward, *Six Thinking Hats,* Boston: Little and Brown, 1985

Eyre, Linda and Richard *Life Balance,* New York: Ballatine Books, 1987

Ferguson, Marilyn, *The Aquaruian Conspiracy,* Los Angeles: J. P. Tarcher, 1980

Gelatt, H. B., ''Positive Uncertainty: A New Decision Making Framework for Counseling'' in *Journal of Counseling Psychology,* Vol. 36, No. 2, 252-256. 1989

Goldberg, Philip, *The Intuitive Edge,* Los Angeles: J. P. Tarcher, 1983.

Golde, Roger, *Muddling Through,* New York: AMACOM, 1976

Janis, Irvin and Leon Mann, *Decision Making,* New York: Free Press, 1977

Kaufmann, Draper, *Teaching The Future:* Palm Springs, California: ETC Publications, 1976

March, James, ''Model Bias in Social Action.'' in *Review of Educational Research,* 42, 413-429. 1975

Michael, Donald, *On Learning To Plan and Planning To Learn,* San Francisco: Josey-Bass Publishers, 1973

Pryor, Hesketh, Robert Pryer and Melanie Gleitzman, ''Making Things Clearer By Making Them Fuzzy: Counseling Illustrations of a Graphic Rating Scale'' *Career Development Quarterly,* Vol. 38, NO. 2, 136–147, 1989. Darlinghurst Australia, 1989.

Taylor, Shelly, *Positive Illusions,* New York: Basic Books, 1989.

Wurman, Richard, *Information Anxiety,* New York: Doubleday, 1989.

NOTES

FOR OTHER FIFTY-MINUTE SELF-STUDY BOOKS
SEE THE BACK OF THIS BOOK.

NOTES

FOR OTHER FIFTY-MINUTE SELF-STUDY BOOKS
SEE THE BACK OF THIS BOOK.

NOTES

NOTES

NOTES

FOR OTHER FIFTY-MINUTE SELF-STUDY BOOKS
SEE THE BACK OF THIS BOOK.

NOTES

FOR OTHER FIFTY-MINUTE SELF-STUDY BOOKS
SEE THE BACK OF THIS BOOK.

ABOUT THE FIFTY-MINUTE SERIES

We hope you enjoyed this book and found it valuable. If so, we have good news for you. This title is part of the best selling *FIFTY-MINUTE Series* of books. All *Series* books are similar in size and format, and identical in price. Several are supported with training videos. These are identified by the symbol **ⓥ** next to the title.

Since the first *FIFTY-MINUTE* book appeared in 1986, millions of copies have been sold worldwide. Each book was developed with the reader in mind. The result is a concise, high quality module written in a positive, readable self-study format.

FIFTY-MINUTE Books and Videos are available from your distributor. A free current catalog is available on request from Crisp Publications, Inc., 95 First Street, Los Altos, CA 94022.

Following is a complete list of *FIFTY-MINUTE Series* Books and Videos organized by general subject area.